UNLEASH
THE WARRIOR
WITHIN

Kelly —

Thank you for being
you. Fly High &
unleash your inner
warrior.

Love,

Katy

KATHY WHITE

Follow Kathy White

Social Media Outlets:

Facebook: @coachkathywhite
Instagram: @coachkathywhite
Email: kathy@vrwaffles.com

Dedication

This book is dedicated to my parents, who taught me how to laugh and who did the best they knew how. I love you both with all my heart.

To my children, Kienna & Lawson, who taught me unconditional love. You are my heart.

To my ride or die, Angie, aka Crackers, who has been by my side for the last 15 years. You can always eat crackers in my bed.

CONTENTS

Acknowledgments

Writing a book has been more challenging than I thought, yet more rewarding and healing than I could have ever imagined. None of this could have been possible without the encouragement of my husband, Jeffery Ertmann. Thank you for loving and supporting me every step of the way.

Kienna Roe Villaplana – Thank you for your fun and spontaneous personality. You genuinely have a gift to make others laugh.

Lawson Roe – Thank you for your wisdom and calmness when life gets so stressful. You are wiser than your young years.

Mom, Malinda White – Thank you for teaching me how to serve others and accept what life throws at me. I can't wait to jump on clouds with you in heaven.

Dad, Darrel White – Thank you for showing me that people can change. You are an amazing father and I am grateful to call you mine.

Mikkel Roe – Thank you for our two beautiful children, Kienna & Lawson. I am grateful for the life that we shared.

Jodi White – Prince and Moon Boots will always remind me of you.

David White – My torn ACL was worth every minute of me dunking you in the lake.

Denise Nicholson – Thank you for helping me find my story and for holding space for me to cry when I shared my story with you. This process was very healing.

Mr. Les Brown – you truly are an inspiration in my life. You have helped me laugh through my cancer journey, and the Power Voice platform catapulted me to writing this book. "The World Needs Your Voice" has been repeated numerous times while writing this book, when it became too much to bear, but I know that if it only helps one person, then it was worth it. I am forever grateful.

Jon Talarico – through your mentoring and coaching, you have truly changed my life. Thank you.

Ian Harvey – thank you for believing in me when I didn't have faith in myself. It only took nine months to get the belief instilled in me.

Dolly Cina – Thank you for showing me the yellow brick road and a whole new world of possibilities. The Universe always has a plan.

Angie Curtis – from being told that we were the bad dance moms to healing through our divorces together and almost getting killed by bison, you and I were always meant to be in each other's lives. Thank you for all our adventures together, for listening, and for giving me life advice.

Foreword

Nobody in life is a stranger to adversity. No matter where you come from, I can guarantee you have faced many obstacles and challenges during your journey. And while we have all struggled, some people are dealt far worse cards than others. A trust-fund baby will rarely experience the pain felt by an orphaned child in a third-world slum. But the truth of the matter is that EVERYONE faces adversity, big or small. Nobody is exempt from the harsh realities that life throws at us.

That was kind of depressing, but bringing down the mood is the furthest thing from my intentions. It is, however, important to understand the unexpectedness and unfairness of life. Nobody asks for the adversity given to them. Some people are born into it, while others experience it further down the road. But it is not the adversity we face that defines us, but instead how we respond to the challenges at hand.

Fight or flight response is a topic much discussed in science and social circles, but I feel that it is missing a key aspect: acceptance. This isn't a good type of acceptance, like acknowledging you have an addiction. Instead, this type of acceptance is a dangerous path that leads to stunted personal growth. I have written and spoken about this theme a lot, and it truly troubles me how many people choose this third option when faced with adversity. Instead of dealing with their troubles, or running away from them, these people accept that these challenges are a part of their life. Instead of working to make their situation better, they simply coast through life, adapting to their obstacles but never conquering them.

This is a very dangerous habit to fall into.

Each and every one of you has a warrior within. When faced with adversity, you may choose to run away or simply live with it. Please let me tell you, you are so much better than that. Everybody on earth has the skills, courage, and strength to conquer their demons. As you will find in this book, all it takes is to unleash the warrior within.

I absolutely love this book, and its message is one that I scream from the rooftops. The pages to come will both pull at your heartstrings and motivate you, all in the confines of one book. *Unleashing the Warrior Within* uses a story of overcoming adversity to teach an invaluable lesson: we all have what it takes.

I feel greatly honored to have my words preface this incredible book, and it is important to me that you head into this book with an open mind and open heart. We all have read articles and even books without retaining a single piece of information, skimming through just for the heck of it. Trust me, you will want to remember this one. So soak in every lesson and moral you can and learn how to unleash the warrior buried inside you.

Do this, and you will accomplish remarkable feats.

You have something special; you have GREATNESS in you.

Les Brown.

Speaker, Author, Trainer.

Introduction

I honor you for reading this book. Have you ever been to that place where you don't know if you care anymore; care about life, care about living?

It was 2009, and I was at my daughter's dance competition at one of the local high schools. I recall sitting in the bleachers with my best friend Angie, aka "Crackers," and she looked at me and asked if I was okay. I nodded and said yes and questioned why she asked this. This year had been incredibly hard. At the time, I thought it was the worst year of my life as my marriage was in shambles. Her response was, "Your eyes look empty." My eyes were empty. My soul was empty. My heart was empty. I had always been able to "fake" being happy, and my happiness was always superficial and surface level. I went through the motions of taking care of my kids, family, household, and work duties.

I was broken for years. I didn't know how to love myself. I was a people pleaser and as a result, I often took on too much and caused anxiety in my life. I gave others the responsibility of making me happy. I had the patience of an angered wasp. I put everyone else's needs in front of my own and took no time for myself.

I was successful by other people's definition of success, based on what they saw as their version of me, but I was empty inside and I didn't know how to change. I read books, went to counseling and seminars, but nothing seemed to help me.

I thought this was my lot in life. Depression and anxiety run in my family. I used to come home from school to find my mom on the couch sleeping for hours. I thought it was a normal part of life. I knew no different.

One day I was driving home from work and thought to myself – *Is this all that life is?* Wake up. Drive to work. Work. Drive Home. Make Dinner. Go to Bed. Repeat. I felt like a robot. I thought to myself that there had to be more in life than this.

I learned to put a shell around my heart and not let people close to me throughout my life. If they don't get close to me, then I can't get hurt. Sound familiar? As I gradually progress through my journey of self-discovery, the shell is breaking into pieces.

I know for that reader that is going through a dark time, some of the things I advise doing are not easy. I encourage you to start small. There are questions and exercises at the end of this book for you to ask yourself and do for yourself. Some will be harder than others and some questions you just might not feel worthy to answer right now. Let me tell you this -- You are loved. You deserve to be happy. You are worthy of attaining the life you want. Use this book to help you heal and gain the joy in your life.

*"Forgiveness is not an occasional act;
it is a constant attitude."*

— Martin Luther King Jr.

CHAPTER 1

Anniversary Dinner – Heartbreak #1

I learned, at a very young age, that I needed to be a quiet and a perfect child, or else the yelling would begin. Kids were to be seen and not heard. This was the motto that was apparent in our household. My dad, who towered over everyone, being 6 foot 2 inches, was the man of the house, and everyone knew that. I could sense when he pulled into the driveway if he had had a good or bad day at a very early age. If it had been a good day, we could still watch the TV shows we wanted and continue being children. If it had been a bad day, you knew to be quiet and avoid joking with him at all costs. I learned this as a way of life.

I have blocked out parts of my past, as it's tough to go back; the pain is sometimes too much to bear. Yet, I know full well that in order to heal my wounds, whether emotional or physical, I must confront even the most painful moments of my past.

When I was a child, my parents' fights could suck the oxygen out of a room. They were vicious and destructive. I witnessed everything from name-calling and insults to physical aggression and verbal jabs. The jabs would consist of both of them lashing out at one another. As a result, there were few peaceful nights in our household. Instead, the high-conflict home brought a sense of sadness. It was very common to find me hiding in my room when these fights escalated. Once the battle (most commonly yelling) started, I would head to my bedroom crying, plugging my ears with my fingers, and hiding behind my closed door.

One evening when I was eight years old, my mom was in a great mood. That day was a special one - it was my parents' anniversary. She was making jokes, dancing, and playing with us kids. My mom, beaming with delight, had decided that tonight she would surprise my dad by making his favorite meal.

She started cooking dinner around 5 pm as my dad always arrived home from work by 5:30, like clockwork. He would generally walk through the door, grab a beer, and then sit down on his chair so he could decompress. Of course, it would be a special treat if he allowed us, kids, to drink a swallow of his beer.

This evening was different. You could feel something was just not right. We glanced at the clock, and it was 5:30 pm but there was no sign of my dad. My dad's delay in coming home seemed odd, but my mom continued happily with her cooking and asked us, children, to set the table.

We finished setting the table and the time was now 5:45 pm. The aroma of dinner was wafting throughout the house; 5:45 pm comes and goes. Dinner was almost done because we ate around 6:00 pm every night, like clockwork.

I felt a shift in my mom's mood. Although she tried to hide her sadness at my dad's absence, there was something different about this night. Then, finally, the big hand on the living room clock ticks to 6:00 pm, and there is still no sign of my dad. My mom had us kids sit down at the table while she completed the finishing touches for dinner.

I remember hearing sniffling sounds coming from the kitchen. They were coming from my mom. I looked over at her, and she had tears rolling down her face. She was talking to herself under her breath. We asked her if she was okay. She replied with shakiness in her voice and heartache that I hadn't seen before. She couldn't believe that he had forgotten that it was their anniversary.

It was now 6:10 pm, and my mom had us start to eat dinner. *The slower we eat, the better*, we thought. At this time, my mom was so upset that she couldn't eat. Tears were rolling down her face. We gave her a big bear hug and told her that we loved her. She thanked us, gave us all hugs and told us that she loved us too.

It was 6:20 pm, and my dad finally stumbled in the door, drunker than I have ever seen him. He tells us that he stopped at the local bar and said he lost track of time. I looked at him with disgust, as I knew how much my mom was hurting. I don't recall if this was a regular occurrence for him, but I remember the hurt I felt that night. He stumbled up the stairs and walked into the kitchen. We all looked up at him in disbelief. How could he hurt our mom like this?

The rest of the night, time went by so fast, but yet so slow.

My mom and dad started yelling at each other. But, this time, it was different than other times. It was like watching the worst verbal boxing match of all time. All of us kids were sitting at the dinner table, watching the verbal jabs flying back and forth. I was 8 years old, so the only thing I understood was that my mom was hurting, which hurt me. My first heartbreak in life was knowing that my dad wasn't the perfect man I imagined him to be, and the pain that I saw in my mom's eyes that night was more than any eight-year-old could handle.

My dad had made it up the stairs and was standing by the stove. The yelling between both of them continued. Then, my mom picked up her cherished Corningware plate, threw it across the kitchen, aiming for my dad. Instead, the plate flew across the kitchen, missed him, hit the cupboard, and shattered into a million pieces.

My sister went running for the phone to make the phone call that might have changed our lives. She quickly dialed our aunt's number, and told her what was transpiring at the house while trying to avoid the yelling. Finally, my aunt and uncle came over and hauled us kids over to a family friend's house. We hadn't been taken to someone's house before, even during all of the volatility in our environment, so we knew that something was different this time.

Our friend had just received what was the hottest toy at the time, The Magic 8 Ball. Being children who didn't always get the most desirable and popular toys, we were excited to use this magic genie. The Magic 8 Ball had the answer to all of life's questions. With a shake of the ball, it would answer anything that you asked of it.

My siblings and I all took turns asking the Magic 8 ball if our parents would get divorced. In 1980, it was not common to get divorced. It was more common and accepted to live in an unhappy marriage than to get divorced. The answers we each received were different, but we each interpreted the answer how we saw fit. My sister wanted them to get divorced, my brother and I did not. Even though I was angry with my dad, I still loved him and wanted him as a part of my life.

I don't know what happened at the house that night with my parents and aunt and uncle, but I know that my parents decided to stay together. My dad quit drinking, and we went to family counseling. Going to counseling was pretty much a laughable event, as no one wanted to be there. Still, my mom was trying to keep her family together.

From the events of that night, plus other verbal boxing matches, we all judged my dad and treated him poorly. I have a lot of regret for the way I treated him when I was a teenager. I was very dismissive of him and would always take my mom's side in any argument they had. I can only imagine how he felt coming home to a house where no one cared if he was there or not. He was out trying to provide an income for the family, and we were ungrateful at home.

I have learned, through my healing journey, that he was broken inside and didn't know how to love. He was doing the best that he knew how to do at this time. Even with the up and down emotions of having my parents in a tumultuous relationship, I still love my parents with all my heart. Unfortunately, my mom passed away in 2011. I miss her dearly every day. She had a personality that lit up the room when she walked in. She made life fun. Her nickname for me when I was a child was George. I don't know why, but I miss it.

To release the warrior within you, you must forgive yourself, and others, so that you can move into the future with a clean slate. Hurt people hurt people, whether intentionally or not. Think about the people in your life that you feel have wronged you somehow. Have you looked at their lives and all the events that have transpired to make them who they are today? During my healing journey, I had to take a step back and look at my dad's life and the hurts he had experienced to understand why he is the way he is. I am not saying that his actions were right, nor am I saying my mom was perfect. I am asking you to take a step back, look at the life of this person who wronged you, and see what hurts they had to endure.

Do you forgive others? If yes, do you let it go after you forgive them, or does the issue come back in your life? Have you forgiven yourself for anything you've done that doesn't align with your beliefs? Whoever needs your forgiveness, forgive them and forgive yourself.

Take some time to recall five different situations in which you blamed others for something that happened to you; find that one big hurt that you have that you want to forgive. Write a forgiveness letter to the owner of the hurt. Feel the emotions and write them down on paper. My suggestion is to hand write this letter and not type it; there is healing when it comes to writing. After you do this, have a burning ceremony. Go outside, put the paper in a fire pit, and burn your hurts (carefully and safely).

"You are braver than you believe, stronger than you seem, and smarter than you think. But the most important thing is, even if we're apart...I'll always be with you."

— A.A. Milne

CHAPTER 2

Always Alone

I could do no wrong. My sister, without fail, would get into trouble by pushing the limits, with limits being anything from yelling at my mom or stealing her prized heirloom jewelry, to smoking at the age of twelve. My brother, being the youngest and the only boy, was favored by both my parents.

I feel as if I raised myself since my parents were emotionally unavailable; my mom was depressed and my dad was angry. Neither of them wanted to be together. My sister didn't make it any easier, and my brother was busy being a rambunctious boy.

When I would come home from school, I would find my mom asleep on the couch most days. Sometimes my friends would try and sit on the sofa, thinking it was a big lump of blankets when in reality, it was my mom sleeping away the agony of her life. She had severe scoliosis and had nearly all her vertebrae fused which put her body in constant pain.

I had a lot of bitterness towards my mom. I yearned for a mom who would sit down with me, hug me, and just say those three words, "I Love You." But, instead, during my teen years, when I needed her most, she was emotionally unavailable to be the mother I needed and wanted.

I was in 7th grade, babysitting for family friends, Bill and Cindy. Bill and my dad worked together for the same company. Unfortunately, the company that they worked for decided to shut their plant here in Utah. They gave their employees the option of early retirement or moving back east to work in their main headquarters. We decided, as a family, not to move. I know my life would be different if we had moved, as I wouldn't be writing this story for you to read right now. I have wondered if life would have been easier or not. Hindsight is always 20/20. My dad had to get two jobs to make sure we had enough money to pay the mortgage and utilities.

I remember being on state assistance, getting food stamps, and getting free lunch at school. During the 1980s, we had physical lunch tickets. Each day you exchanged your ticket for school lunch. It was very embarrassing to hear, over the loudspeaker, "Kathy White, please come to the office to pick up your free lunch tickets." The looks and feelings, whether imagined or not, are difficult for a teenager.

The house was eerily quiet during this time, as my dad was never at home, and the severity of my mom's depression and sleeping increased. Then, my sister got pregnant at fifteen, and all hell broke loose in the house.

I had just come home one evening and started heading up the stairs when I heard the start of yet another verbal boxing match. I thought to myself, *what did I walk into now?* This argument was between my sister and my dad. It was common for both of them to yell at each other and sometimes even get into physical altercations. Sometimes, it was about how my sister treated my mom during her teenage years. Other times, it was about something that my Dad said, or did, that my sister disagreed with. Occasionally, my dad would yell at my mom, so my sister would play interference.

This particular afternoon turned out to be the pinnacle of the verbal boxing matches. The culmination of the game ended with my sister yelling at our dad and saying, as a matter of fact, "Well, you are not my father, so you can't tell me what to do." I looked at her with disbelief. Dumbfounded and heartbroken, I said, "Yes, he is." She proceeded to tell me that she had to get her birth certificate because of getting pregnant. The biological father on her birth certificate was not our dad. Our parents had lied to us for fifteen years, even to the extent that they pretended they were married for one more year than they actually were. When I questioned my dad about it recently, he couldn't remember why they had chosen to lie to us about the years they were married. At the time, it made sense.

After my sister had her baby, life at the house was still stressful, but not nearly as bad. I could drive at this time, so I could always get away with my friends or go to work. Plus, we had a cute new baby in the household to love and adore. Yelling still went on. I thought this was how everyone lived. My mom was still depressed, and my dad was still angry. No one truly cared if I was at the house or not. Being a teenager, and disinterested in staying at home, I would go out with my friends, but I never liked going to parties.

Then, my sister got married to the father of her child and had another child. They had to move out of state because he joined the military. They took away the things that had made life tolerable at the house, my nephew and niece.

I felt invisible. If I was a good child, then no one seemed to notice me. If I was a bad child, then I got the attention I so desperately needed. I chose to be a good child and went on with life. I went to school, worked, and aimed to get good grades. Because no one seemed to care if I was home or not, I didn't have a curfew. Most kids would jump at the idea of no curfew, and although it did have its advantages, it still would have been nice for someone to care if I was home by a specific time.

I was in the choir during my high school years. However, my parents never came to a single one of my performances throughout all of high school. I felt that my parents didn't love me; otherwise they would have chosen to attend at least one of my concerts throughout my high school career.

Have there been times in your life when you have felt utterly alone? During my teenage years, I felt incredibly alone, depressed, and unloved. To feel fulfilled and loved, we all need a sense of community. A sense of community can come from anywhere, such as your neighborhood, family, church, and friends.

Your experiences can be your most incredible power. A lot of people use their pasts as their prison; I know I did. My heart was in jail. Someone had locked it up and removed the key and I didn't know how to unlock it. I thought I had been given an unfair lot in life with having an angry father and depressed mother as a child. I have now learned that this is my most significant power. Growing up, all I wanted was for my parents' eyes to light up when I walked into the room. I never felt seen, heard, or honestly that I even mattered. Please don't get me wrong; I am not criticizing my parents because they didn't know any different. It took me a long time to understand this concept.

If you are reading this, I want you to know that in order to release your inner warrior, you need to know that you, and your story, matter. Sometimes, we feel like our traumas are no big deal when you are on the other side of your healing journey. But, I promise you that whatever you've been through, someone out there needs to hear your story.

If you feel alone, reach out to someone, and let them know how you are feeling. It can be anyone from a family member, friend or counselor, to a fellow church member. The number one thing I do when I feel a sense of sadness is to volunteer. Volunteering brings happiness as you are focusing on someone or something other than yourself. Find something you are passionate about and commit to volunteering once a week. If that's too much, then do once a month. If that's too much, do once a quarter. Just commit to volunteering and you will find that you are not as sad or feel as alone anymore.

Joy does not simply happen to us.
We have to choose joy and keep choosing
it every day.

CHAPTER 3

Never Good Enough

I have a fear of not being accepted or, in other words, being rejected. Growing up in Utah in the 1970s, almost everyone was a "Latter-Day Saint" or, as most people say, "Mormons." However, my family was one of probably four families in the neighborhood that were not Mormons. When I was in Kindergarten, I recall running home, crying. I opened the door, and my mom looked at me and asked me what was wrong. I told her I had no friends and none of the kids would play with me because I wasn't Mormon. Although it seems silly now, being a child and not having friends to play with was hard.

When I felt so alone during my teenage years, I joined the Mormon Church. I felt that I would be accepted more if I were of the same religion as my peers. Certain parts of the Mormon culture did give me that community and connection. However, I left the Mormon Church when I was twenty, as I genuinely didn't believe in its teachings.

I was on the swim team from the ages of 8 to 12. I never had upper arm strength as a child and always came in 5th or 6th place at all the swim meets. Finally, it got so embarrassing that no one would even cheer for me at the end of the lane as they knew I would never be in the first place position. Not having anyone cheer for me made me feel not good enough.

During Elementary and Junior High School, I was always one of the last kids picked for sports activities. I am sure it stemmed from my physical form of being incredibly skinny, not being Mormon, and being the dreaded girl. If you are reading this and think that I am being hard on the Utah Mormon culture, I urge you to find someone who felt like an outcast in Utah and see if their stories relate. I assure you they will.

Kids at school told me all the time I was ugly. When you already feel uncomfortable in your body, this is hard to hear. I only contemplated committing suicide once, and that was in 10th grade. It was a fleeting moment as, for whatever reason, I always had the drive to be better than I was the day before. It wasn't until I got older that I understood and accepted that I am beautiful.

My personality is shy and quiet. Because of this, people tend to misjudge me. For example, one day, I heard a couple of boys yelling my name at our local grocery store. As I hear, "Kathy," I turn towards them, they then proceeded to call me a "bitch". Unfortunately, neither one of these boys knew the real me. They only knew the "me" that they saw in the classroom. I already had low self-esteem and being called a "bitch" made me feel horrible.

Were you ever bullied as a child? Adolescent? Adult? When I was four years old, I vividly recall sitting in our front yard with my mom and the neighbor lady, Karen (one of my mom's friends). Karen always made fun of me – how I looked, what I wore, what I did, what I said, what I didn't say. You name it; she would tease me about it, thinking she was funny. I think it was because I was the quiet one, so she figured it was okay to pick on me. In her mind, I was defenseless. That day, Karen grabbed a handful of grass and shoved it down my shirt, and then started laughing at me because I couldn't defend myself. After that, Karen persistently set out to humiliate me, intimidate me, or scare me whenever she could.

One of my first jobs was as a data entry clerk for a man named Arthur. He was mean, a micro-manager, and very arrogant. I had never met a businessman from New York City prior to this. What an eye-opener for me this was, as I was a naïve Utah teenager just wanting the experience. I was shocked that my dream to be in the business world meant I had to endure the insults Arthur dished out daily. I became good friends with his assistant. However, she complained about him every moment she could. Finally, one day, she decided to quit as she had had enough of his criticism. When she left, I had the task of taking on her responsibilities as well as my own. I chose to endure for the next few weeks. The straw that broke the camel's back was when Arthur came to me and asked, "Are we placating you enough today?" Which meant: are we giving you enough praise today? I thought it incredibly rude and unprofessional of him. I left that night and never went back.

I found my gender disadvantageous while in the workplace, specifically in management positions. Being a female working in Utah, you are paid less than your male counterparts (even with the same education/experience). Once I was exposed to this unfairness and inequality, it made me angry. Utah is ranked #50 in male vs. female pay equality in the United States. (Source: https://www.business.org/hr/benefits/gender-pay-gap/). I wanted to get paid equal to my male counterparts as I had either the same or more experience than they had.

I had received my Bachelor's degree in Accounting, had a few years of Accounts Payable and leadership experience under my belt, and wanted to get into more of a Supervisor AP role. A large online retailer had advertised an AP Assistant Manager role at a specific salary amount. I met all the criteria, plus I already had a year of experience at the company, so I interviewed for the job. The hiring manager offered me the job but at a lower salary than the one that had been advertised. I spoke to several business leaders who all advised me not to take the offer. They all felt that there was no reason why I shouldn't get the same salary as published. Unfortunately, the hiring manager was that stereotypical Utah Mormon male that looked down upon females in the work environment. Being in many leadership roles in Utah throughout my life, I have seen this repeat itself, not only with me, but other females in the Utah business world.

I have developed a strong will to prove people wrong and myself right. It has developed over the years of being exposed to, and believing, all of these limiting ideas about myself. "You are not the right religion, not the proper gender, ugly, fat, depressed." You name it.

You can do whatever you want to do. People judge others by the feeling of smallness within themselves. When people are bullying you or criticizing you, it is not you. It is 100 percent them and how they feel about themselves. Even if they seem like they are confident, I assure you, somewhere they are hurting. If they weren't hurting, they wouldn't be treating others poorly.

It is okay not to fit in. I used to think that I needed to be of the correct gender, same religion, the perfect weight, or look a certain way for others to like and accept me. I found that in order to start unlocking my heart's prison, I needed to be true to myself. Sometimes it's hard, especially as we are constantly bombarded by ads depicting unrealistic ideas of how females are "supposed" to look. The best thing that I have ever done in life is to accept myself, no matter what, and let everything else go. The people who choose to like me, for me, will stay. The ones that have left had their part of my life journey, and it's okay that they left.

"You begin to fly when you let go of self-limiting beliefs and allow your mind and aspirations rise to greater heights."

— Brian Tracy

CHAPTER 4

Moonbeam
- Heartbreak #2

I met Mike, the father of my children, when I was a junior in high school. We attended the same high school and were both Police Cadets together. Being a silly teenager, I stole his watch one day in class. After that, I always looked forward to our talks. Mike had a way of telling a story that captivated an audience.

Being in charge of the ride-along schedule for police cadets, Mike always scheduled us together to do vacation property checks on houses. I was naïve enough to believe, and it was partly true, that he needed guidance with his girl drama. One day, after a Dutch dinner at Wendy's and a stroll at the local park, we had gone over to his house. That night we were again talking about his "girl drama," so in my mind, I didn't know he had feelings for me. I was always the friend to the guys but never the girlfriend. I was easy to talk to, but no one wanted to date me. We were standing on the grass when he took my hand, pulled me close, kissed me, and our relationship started. We got married two years later.

I didn't want to have children. I had lived in such a volatile and tumultuous household that I didn't want to expose any child to that way of life. I wanted to go to school and focus on my career. I didn't want to bring any child into the unloving environment in which I had grown up. But, as the years went on, I felt that I had more and more of a yearning for children. I did know for sure that I wanted to get my Bachelor's degree before I did anything. One of my paradigms in life is that I don't finish what I start, but getting my degree was entirely within my control.

Whenever I desired children, I would have my niece and nephew come over for a night or the weekend. Of course, they fought like siblings, so that was enough to squash any desire of wanting any little kids running around for a while.

I initially set out to get a degree in Social Justice. I have a huge heart and a desire to help people, especially those who have difficulty helping themselves. I spoke with my Police Cadet advisor and told him that this was the path I wanted to pursue. He replied that if I followed this field, it would hurt my heart since it is so pure, and I couldn't un-see what I would see. Feeling defeated, I decided to go into Elementary education instead and started my studies at the local community college. I was almost done with my degree when I realized that this path wasn't right for me. So, knowing full well that I would have to add one year, if not two, to get my degree, I made a huge change. I went on to get my Business Degree from Salt Lake Community College (SLCC) and my Accounting degree from the University of Utah (U of U).

While focusing on my education, Mike became a police officer and started a career at West Valley City Police Department. I received my Bachelor's degree in 1996 from the U of U. My mental wellbeing couldn't have handled another day of school. I chose not to get my Master's at that time, knowing full well that if I wanted to become a Certified Public Accountant (CPA), I would have to go back to school.

We moved into a starter home that we intended on selling in a couple of years in West Jordan, Utah. Life was good. We were happy on the outside but still struggling with our internal demons of unhappiness on the inside.

We decided about six months before my graduation that we would try to get pregnant. The first moon cycle (period) comes, and I am devastated. Second moon cycle, and I am more devastated. The third moon cycle doesn't come, and I am ecstatic. We had waited a long time to get pregnant. I used a pregnancy test, and there was a faint line indicating that yes, we were pregnant; to be sure, we found a doctor that could do a blood test. He completed the test and confirms that YES! We are pregnant. After six years of waiting, we were filled with joy and on cloud nine. We told our families, friends, you name it; we told everyone we were pregnant. Everyone was happy for us.

A few weeks went by, and I started bleeding. As I had never been pregnant before, I didn't know if this was normal or not. I had a knot in the bottom of my stomach, telling me something wasn't right. We headed back to the doctor, and he completed another blood test. He informed us that the pregnancy hormone has now diminished in my bloodstream, so the blood I saw was a miscarriage. My heartbreak number two in life was having a miscarriage. I felt a sense of sadness like I hadn't felt before. Why me? These evil thoughts played throughout my mind. Was I not good enough to be a mother? We had to call our family then and tell them the news. I cried for days, days that turned into nights. People who didn't know would offer congratulations, and then the crying would start again. I felt rejected, yet again, in my life. We were blessed with two exceptional children years later, Kienna and Lawson.

Miscarriage grief is real and is not related to how long you were pregnant. Miscarriage grief is related to your bond with your baby. Unfortunately, miscarriage grief is not acknowledged. "A miscarriage is a psychologically challenging event. Unlike the loss of other family members, the grieving individual has had few direct life experiences or actual times with the deceased to review, remember, and cherish. There is no publicly acknowledged person to bury or established rituals to structure mourning and gain support, and, often, relatively few opportunities are present to express thoughts and feelings about the loss due to the secrecy that often accompanies the early stages of pregnancy. When others do know about the loss, they often fail to appreciate its impact or minimize it, making comments such as, 'It was not meant to be' or 'It is for the best.'" –Norman Brier, Ph.D., "Grief Following Miscarriage: A Comprehensive Review of the Literature," Journal of Women's Health, 2008, vol. 17, p.451-464

Have you felt rejected in your life? Do you think that no matter what you do, it is never good enough? As a child, teenager, and young adult, I felt rejected wherever I turned.

Rejection is the step between you and your next opportunity in life. Rejection hurts, and it's okay to feel those emotions. However, rejection doesn't have to hold you back. If you feel rejected, allow yourself time to process your hurt feelings. In our fast-paced society, it's not acceptable to "be" in your feelings. Society tells us that we need to "get over" our emotions, and it's not okay to feel, cry, or even throw a temper tantrum on the ground.

Make a list of positive qualities that you possess. Then, find a mirror, look at yourself and repeat these qualities in the present tense while looking at yourself. For example, "I am beautiful." Be in the moment while looking at yourself in the mirror. Looking at your beautiful self and connecting with the real you is hard for most people that struggle with self-image issues, but keep doing it. Eventually, your goal will be 15 minutes of self-reflection to remind yourself that you are loved.

"Sometimes rejection in life is redirection."

— Unknown

CHAPTER 5

Lost boy

Life went on, and I became a mother, wife, and accountant. I used to define myself by these titles. Mike was still doing police work but was learning that it was hard on his mental well being.

Being a police officer's wife, you see a different side to your husband than others do. Police Officers see, and deal with, some of the most horrific and damaging situations day in and day out. We were both told to wait to get married, as Mike would change. Neither one of us believed it, as we were young and in love. There is no way a person can remain unchanged when constantly seeing children die, nightly drug busts, and always having to watch your back because you want to go home to your family. At times, I feel that people expect police officers to have no feelings, no family or friends. I understand it is their choice to become police officers, but they are people too.

In Utah, counseling sessions for police officers weren't mandatory back in the 1990s. Sadly, police officers are perceived as weak when they need to get counseling. As a result, their peers or supervisors look down upon them when they attend counseling sessions, sometimes even preventing promotions. Additionally, I found those police counselors were untrained in treating PTSD, which is a risk for all first responders and their family members.

With permission from Mike, here is an example of a call he has experienced.

July 21st, 1996

1521hrs 7/21/1996 102°:

"Valley 12 Copy lost child."

"Valley 12, go ahead."

"Valley 12 Copy lost child... 2-year-old Caucasian male last seen two hours ago wearing a white t-shirt, tan shorts, blonde hair, and blue eyes."

"Valley 12 en route"

"It was 41 minutes before the end of my shift, not a big deal. I've had to work overtime before many times. Although it was hot outside under the summer sun, I was kept cool by the air conditioner in my car and the ice-cold beverage in my Big Gulp cup. I had plans with my wife and my in-laws to go to Rocky Mountain Raceway, but that wouldn't be until 7 pm. So I had plenty of time to find the little boy, write my report and enjoy my family time.

Arriving on the scene, I found the scared mother and father in the front yard. I stopped, got further information, asked if they had searched everywhere in the home (often we would find a kid sleeping in the closet... You know... being a kid). They assured me they had and that they and several neighbors were searching the yards in the neighborhood. I assured them we would find him and that he would be okay. I asked his mom to stay at home and asked his dad to continue the search with the neighbors. I told them I would drive further into the neighborhood to search outlying areas, especially around 3100 South. I drove past a dark maroon colored car in the street in front of the home and continued to 3100 South.

After a few minutes of searching, I began driving back towards the home. As I did, several teenagers started running toward me.

"They found him!" But something wasn't right. There was panic on their faces. "He was in the car!"

I floored the accelerator. I could not get to the home fast enough.

"Valley 12, start me another unit and expedite medical!" I shouted into my police radio.

After what felt like an eternity, I arrived seconds later to a group of people circled around the distraught parents and a lifeless child. I ran to the child from my car, noting that the child was not breathing, vomitus was oozing from his mouth, and he was completely blue. His shirt was off, and as I got down on my knees and touched his chest to begin CPR, I reflexively pulled my hand away as his chest felt as hot as a stove. Dad and I continued CPR until medical assistance arrived.

He had been dead for a while, long before I had been dispatched. Finally, medical arrived, along with several officers. Mom was sobbing in anguish; Dad tried to keep his emotion in check as they placed the child into the ambulance. Speaking later to the paramedics, I learned that the only reason they transported the child was to allow his Dad to believe he tried to save his life.

I had to keep my emotions in check. There still an investigation to do. Was this an accident? Was this intentional? Was there negligence involved by the parents?

My investigation found the child had climbed into the car in front of their home to play with his five-year-old brother. Being children, they pretended they were driving the vehicle. The five-year-old got hot and left the car. The two-year-old was not strong enough to get out of the car after his brother left, so he passed out on the back seat and died due to the car's internal temperature.

The temperature reading inside the car was 132 degrees. The child's internal temperature at the hospital thirty minutes later was 116 degrees. He baked to death in that car, and all he wanted to do was pretend... just what every child does...pure innocence, and he died from it.

There was something that broke inside of me that day. I knew I'd never be the same, and I have never been. I cried inside for fifteen years. It destroyed my marriage and what I knew as "my family," it ruined my career. It nearly destroyed me in 2009 when I attempted suicide. The pain I suffered from being a cop and seeing that lifeless child, baked from the heat of the car, was just too much to bear." – Mike Roe

The above is one of many examples all honest police officers have as one of their daily calls. Of course, some police officers can handle these experiences better than others.

I was with Mike for over twenty years. I spent numerous years with him, walking on eggshells, even before this incident, thinking he would commit suicide as he so often threatened to do. I was scared. I didn't want to break up my family, nor did I want to lose him. He kept telling me that we (me and the kids) would be better off without him. Take the insurance money. He even plotted how to kill himself so that the insurance company wouldn't suspect him of committing suicide. (There is a clause in most insurance policies that suicide voids the policy.)

Throughout the years, as he fought with his internal demons, he would fall into a very dark place and threaten suicide. I would feel bad and talk him out of it. He would be fine, for a while, and then something would trigger it again. This was the cycle we were in.

In 2009, Mike was selling his Glock pistol so we could get money to pay the mortgage. I wasn't worried because his dad raised him with firearms; Mike was on the SWAT team and a firearms instructor while at the police department. So I didn't think much of it when he left that morning.

He left around 9 am and was supposed to be home by 10 am. By 11:30 am, I was getting anxious. I sent him a text; no response. I called him; no answer. It wasn't like him not to answer a text or a phone call. Something was wrong. In my mind, I thought he finally did the unthinkable. I started crying and couldn't stop. Feeling distraught, I called his family to see if they knew where he was. No one knew where he was. I started processing how I would handle living life as a widow—paying the mortgage—raising two children—providing food. It was all racing through my mind. Finally, his brother found him midafternoon in the Home Depot parking lot, contemplating killing himself again. Once he got home, I felt relieved. But, as time went on, I found myself angry. I was hurting inside. I thought about how unfair it was that I had to deal with this roller coaster of emotions. I tried for over 20 years, and I couldn't do it anymore.

I had my issues with depression, and so did he. Different situations would send us to either couples counseling or individual counseling. None of which I truly felt worked. I don't know if it was the counselors or us not putting in our 100 percent. As always, hindsight is 20/20.

Looking back at it, a lot of my anger stemmed from him always threatening to commit suicide. He felt that it would be better for everyone left behind. I blamed a lot of my unhappiness on him, my parents, and my childhood. I was playing the blame game, not realizing it was my responsibility to own my emotions.

You are one hundred percent in charge of your thoughts, feelings, and actions. Thoughts, feelings, and actions are the choices you make. Val Van De Wall wrote, "When a person takes responsibility for their life and the results they are obtaining, they will cease to blame others as the cause of their results. Since you cannot change other people, blame is inappropriate. Blaming others causes a person to remain bound in a prison of their own making. When you take responsibility, blame is eliminated, and you are free to grow."

Have you ever felt lost in life? That no one is out there for you? Or can no one love you because you are unlovable? I felt unlovable for most of my life. I was always playing second fiddle to my older sister or younger brother. Yes, the blame game of the middle child. Do you blame others for your life? I thought others were to blame for my unhappiness. I gave my power away to them. When my dad, mom, or Mike had a bad day that would mean I had a bad day as well. It is okay to hold space for others when they have challenging times, but you don't have to let their emotions project onto you. Some people expect this, as they want you to feel the hurt that they feel. Be very conscious of this and set clear boundaries. Remind them that you are there to hold space for them and be there for them, but you will not let their emotional baggage become yours.

If you are having suicidal thoughts, please call or text the National Suicide Hotline at 1-800-273-8255.

"Never let a stumble in the road be the end of the journey."

— Unknown

CHAPTER 6

Razzleberry Pie

It was 2007. We were in the park having a picnic and playing volleyball with our network marketing team. Mike received a phone call from his mom. When he put the phone down; he looked like he had just seen a ghost. His dad, Jack, was not doing well. We asked my sister and her husband to take care of the kids so we could run over to his parent's house to determine what was going on. We ran inside the house to find Jack sitting at the dining room table, eating what would be his last piece of Razzleberry pie.

Jack was dazed and confused, slowly eating and enjoying his piece of delicious pie. Mike switched to cop mode and started talking sternly to his dad and asked him what was going on. I was in the living room, but I could witness everything from where I was standing. Jack started to fidget and wanted to sit on the couch, so Mike assisted him in getting from the kitchen to the living room. Halfway to the living room, Jack fell on the ground and went into cardiac arrest.

I had never witnessed anyone dying before. Mike, fighting back the tears, started practicing CPR on his dad, even though he knew his dad was done with this life and wanted to go. We called the paramedics, who got to the house in impressive time, ran upstairs, and took over doing Jack's CPR. Even though Jack didn't want to live, by law, the paramedics must do CPR until they see a notarized copy of a DNR (Do Not Resuscitate) form. It was frantic in the household. *How can first responders go through this on a daily and nightly basis,* I thought to myself. Emotions were running high. I heard sounds from Jack that sounded like he was about to come back to life, and then he would go again.

Mike and his mother were running desperately through the house, trying to find the DNR that Jack had completed. Mike's mom was about to lose her husband of 49 years. Mike was about to lose his father. I was witnessing all this, not knowing what to do. I felt in the way at this point. Finally, Mike ran upstairs with the book that contained the DNR. As soon as the paramedic read it and made sure it was notarized, CPR ceased immediately. Jack transitioned that night. The paramedics packed up and left Jack on the floor where he had fallen earlier. Now, we had to wait for the funeral home to arrive to pick up his body.

There was something eerie about looking at the dead, lifeless body of the man who was my father-in-law—a man I highly respected and loved. Emotions were running high as the family started gathering at the house. The siblings said their goodbyes to their father and grabbed a sheet to cover his lifeless body.

Piecing things backward, Jack had planned this as the night he was going to transition. I am not sure how, to this day, but I have heard speculation. I know that he purposely went to one of his favorite Salt Lake City restaurants and purchased Razzleberry pie for this occasion.

My sister had dropped our kids off at Mike's parents' house later that evening. It was good for them to be at the house with their dad and grandma during this time. All the siblings would be heading home for the night, and we decided that Lawson and Mike would stay in the house with Mike's mom to make sure she felt safe and was comforted.

Kienna, who was eight at the time, and I, went and got in our car. I began driving east down the street, got to the top of the block, and realized that I had forgotten something at Mike's parents' house. I turned the car around and came to a stop in front of the house. A young adult male, who lived down the street (although I had never seen him before), suddenly appeared by my car window and started yelling at Kienna and me to get out of the car. *How am I supposed to fight off these guys plus protect my child?* I didn't have any weapons in my vehicle. Terrified, as I was not sure what to do, I told Kienna to call her father. Kienna picked up my cell phone and called Mike to come outside.

Mike ran outside and saw the strange guy yelling at me to get out of the car. He loudly yelled at him, "Hey, get away from the car," as he walked up to the male and grabbed him by his right arm. Kienna and I were still in the car with the windows up, shaking uncontrollably.

Mike saw that this man had something in his left front pocket that he was holding and told him to keep his hand in his pocket, as Mike believed he had a gun or knife. Mike heard what sounded like someone approaching behind him, so he turned the guy to his rear. Two males with golf clubs in their hands were walking up to the house. The bigger one of the two was yelling at Mike and telling him that he would knock Mike's head off. Mike yelled at his brother to grab the pistol on the TV as Mike held onto the guy. Mike kicked the guy in the waist when his brother came out, pushing him away from him and grabbing the gun from his brother's hand. Mike then pointed out in their direction and told them that he would shoot if they did not stop coming towards him. They then backed away, saying they were going to kill Mike.

While all this was transpiring, Mike's mother called the police. When they arrived, one police officer wanted to arrest Mike. But, another police officer told him that he best not, as Mike hadn't done anything wrong. The police officer then walked up to the suspects' house and said that if they came down to the house again, Mike would shoot them and that he was legally justified to do so. We found out the following week that the suspects had had a home invasion robbery the prior week. They had thought that my eight-year-old daughter and myself were the suspects coming back to do it again. All three suspects were high on weed and meth that night.

That incident was very traumatic for me but even more so for my eight-year-old daughter. I remember holding her hand, hugging her, and telling her it would be okay. But, unfortunately, this trauma has followed her into her adult life. Regrettably, considering what was going on with losing Jack that night, I didn't think to get Kienna into counseling for this event.

It's okay to be scared, ask for help, and be supported by others when you are uncomfortable. Unfortunately, society shames us for feeling afraid. Fear is a natural emotion, and if you feel scared, allow yourself to acknowledge it. Have you been so afraid to do something, and then afterward you think to yourself, "well, that was no big deal." For me, it was free swimming with sharks and the first time I went skydiving. Those things terrified me, but I accomplished them both, and I will be forever grateful that I took the plunge and did it. I have put off so many things in life because I was "scared." I was scared of what society thought of me, afraid that I wasn't doing it right, terrified that I didn't have enough money, or nervous that I would look silly. But, unfortunately, life is short, my friends. Do Life Scared.

Myles Munroe states, "*The wealthiest place in the world is not the gold mines of South America or the oil fields of Iraq or Iran. It is not the diamond mines of South Africa or the banks of the world. The wealthiest place on the planet is just down the road. It is the cemetery. There lie buried - companies that were never started, inventions that were never made, bestselling books never written, and masterpieces never painted. In the cemetery is buried the greatest treasure of untapped potential.*"

I had to think about that quote. At first, I thought another person could finish this person's poem or book…but that's not what he intended. Instead, Myles Munroe meant that we all had so much in us, ready to give, but then we got scared or life beat us down, and it was OUR books,

OUR songs, OUR poems, that had been placed upon our hearts, that were never finished.

Do you have something that you started and haven't completed? A piece of art? Poem? Book? Wood project? Meditate and think about this project that you know, deep down, would make you come to life if you completed it. Take some time over the next week and if childcare is needed – ask for it. If a day off from work is necessary – ask for it. Take some time for yourself, to get out your soul's desire in physical form. Journal how this accomplishment makes you feel once you complete the project.

"Sometimes what you're most afraid of doing is the very thing that will set you free."

-Unknown

CHAPTER 7

Getting off Track

Do you ever feel that your life is a mess, or that you have caused another person's life to be a mess? I know I did. It was 2009, and our family business was falling apart, and so was our marriage. I started talking to a guy at work, and we connected as I had never connected with someone before. I have no idea why. It could be because I was hurting emotionally from my marriage that was falling apart. It could be because, in a different situation, he could have been my soul mate. I can't tell you why. We had an "emotional" affair, which led to physical contact when my first husband and I were separated. I knew it was wrong, but I was hurting inside, and this was the one thing that was making me feel better.

Mike and I decided to get back together and work on our marriage. I knew I had to tell him what happened. Telling Mike was by far one of the hardest things I have ever had to do. I will never forget the hurt in his eyes. Even with our marriage being in shambles, I never intended to hurt Mike, and for this, I am sorry.

During this time, I was still trying to be the perfect person, which consisted of working, being a business owner, dance mom, basketball mom, wife, daughter, and employee. I thought maybe if I did just a bit more, then I would be happy. But, unfortunately, my inner demon of depression reared its ugly head that year, more so than any other year of my life. My soul was tired. I was tired of fighting the never-winning battle of depression that was my lot in life.

We were required to be at my daughter's dance competitions one hour before they started. This particular day, I felt lifeless. I knew what I was supposed to do and say, but no feelings or emotions came out. It was as if I was a robot shouting out orders to my daughter. "Make sure you have your costumes. Make sure your makeup is on. Make sure your hair is up and curled. Make sure you have a snack."

Kienna and I got in the vehicle and headed over to the local high school. It was not unusual for just the two of us to go to her dance competitions because, honestly, dance competitions are super long and tedious, unless it's that prized two- or three-minute dance out of an entire eight-hour day.

I found Kienna's dance team, dropped her off with her dance coach, and headed over to the bleachers. I was attempting not to catch anyone's eye as I knew it was only a matter of time before the tears would start rolling out of my eyes. I spot my co-team parent, Angie, on the bleachers and walked rapidly through the sea of dance moms. I never did fit into the dance mom scene, so I was easy to spot. Most dance moms are in heels, designer jeans, and a bedazzled shirt. I was in my usual attire of jeans, a hoodie, and boots. This day, I was grateful for my sweatshirt as I could hide behind it.

I didn't want anyone to know I wasn't okay. It wasn't acceptable not to be happy and to cry. I have always been a very emotional person and have been criticized and made fun of for this. I found Angie, and sat down. I'm usually full of conversation, but today was different. I didn't want to talk to her. I didn't want anyone to talk to me. I put my hood over my head to make sure no one could see me, and the lonely tears started dripping down my face. Angie saw me, and realizing that there was something wrong, asked if I was okay. I nodded and said yes and questioned why she asked this. Her response was, "Your eyes look empty." My eyes were empty. My soul was empty. More than anything, my heart was empty.

We all can put a year to some sort of trial we have had in our lives. Think to yourself what year that is for you. Some people can even get to the month, the day, even the minute- and know what that trial is for them.

Do you let yourself hold onto your past? Are you attached to your story? Do you want to heal from your past and use it as a teaching moment instead of a weapon? Have you ever thought to yourself, "Why am I holding onto this if it hurts so much?" Maybe you're afraid of the unknown. Perhaps you believe your pain will protect you. Maybe you think that by holding onto your pain that you will punish the perpetrator.

How do we let go of the past? It's easy for people who haven't gone through our experiences to say, "let it go, don't think about it, it's the past." But, it's hard to learn from those experiences and know they are still part of us without letting them define who we are anymore.

Jim Rohn states, "One of the best ways to approach our feelings about the past is to use it as a school, not as a weapon. It is easy to allow the past to instruct us and increase our value."

It was 2012, and I had just ventured out on my first girls' trip of my entire life. Two of my girlfriends, Angie and Jamie, and I, planned a weekend at Jackson Hole. We would be staying with a family member for the weekend and river rafting on Saturday. We all sounded like giddy teenagers as we were all newly divorced and going on our first solo adventures together.

I printed off the MapQuest directions to Jackson Hole, Wyoming, from Salt Lake City (SLC), Utah. It's a three-hour drive from SLC to Jackson Hole. Angie was driving; I was in the passenger seat or, as others put it, the Co-Pilot seat, and Jamie was in the back seat. I tend to fall asleep in cars. Not once did it go through my mind that I chose this seat so I needed to stay awake. How hard is it to go northeast on the freeway to get to our destination?

We headed east on I-80. I fell asleep not even 30 minutes into our drive. Angie jolted me awake as we go past the Evanston, Wyoming exit (which we were supposed to take) and asked if we are heading in the right direction. Confidently, looking at the directions on MapQuest, I proceed to tell her that it's a bit further.

It's 10 pm, and one of my friends texts me to see if we had arrived safely. I tell him that we have not arrived yet, but I was sure we would be there in no time. He replied, very concerned and worried, that we should have been there by now. Wyoming is not very densely populated, and at this time, GPS didn't work. It was difficult to see any road signs, let alone read them in the black midnight sky. Finally, he said, the next exit you can take – take it.

We pulled into a town called Lander, Wyoming. All three of us walked into the gas station and ask where we are and how to get to Jackson Hole. I recall the gas station attendant vividly saying at the top of her lungs with a bit of a drawl to her voice, "Well, you are in hillbilly hell." We had traveled to the east side of the Teton Mountains, and we were supposed to be on the west side.

Image source: www.mapquest.com

The quickest way to travel to Jackson Hole from Lander, Wyoming, is over the Tetons, through an Indian Reservation, via a two-lane road that was not well maintained. It was 1 am. We were all awake now. We haven't seen anyone else on this road. We had no cell service, and not one person in any of our families would have ever expected us to be in Lander, Wyoming.

We were watching for whites of eyes -- not wanting to hit any animals, as antelope and deer are common in Wyoming. We finally got to the top of the mountain and see not only one set of eyes, but hundreds upon hundreds of spooky sets of eyes. We slowed down, trying to get a grip of what was about to happen. Then, we felt the ground rumbling and stop the car. The car starts shaking. Could it possibly be an earthquake?

We look to our right and see nothing.

We look to our left….and it starts; one running bison, two running bison… ten running bison. Hundreds and hundreds, if not thousands, of running bison, were surrounding us. We were in the middle of a bison stampede!

We started screaming like little schoolgirls as we thought we would die that night by way of a bison stampede.

The bison were running in front of the car, around the vehicle, even behind the car. Everywhere we looked there was another bison. During our entire time on this road, we hadn't seen another vehicle until now. Then, finally, we saw headlights from a truck. Without a care in the world, this man drove through the stampede as if he was out on a Sunday drive.

One of the bison turned towards our car, and we were now in a bison stare-down—three girls in our mid-size vehicle and one bison twice the size of our car. The big eyes of the bison are staring at us while he huffed about, ready to charge the vehicle. After what seems like an eternity, the bison finally got tired of our stare down and rejoined his herd.

After all the bison had crossed the road, we get out of the car, shaking, crying, and laughing. We had just crossed paths with a bison stampede on the top of the Teton Mountains and won.

Think about your life. What is something in your life, "your bison," that is staring you down? Who do you need on your team to get through your stampede? Do they know that you need them? If not, take the time to tell them now. If you have parents that are alive, do you spend time with them? Talk to them on the phone? If you have children, do you spend time playing with them on their level? Do you have deep conversations that they will treasure forever?

I love the song "Cat's in the Cradle" by Harry Chapin. During one of the self-improvement seminars that I attended, they played this song while we all held hands, and then we were to write a letter to our parents. The letter was to consist of love and forgiveness. I encourage you to read the lyrics or even listen to the song and genuinely meditate on these words. If you feel called to write your parents a letter, then do so. When my mom passed, I didn't have any regrets as I had written this love letter of understanding, forgiveness, and apology.

"Even if you're on the right track, you'll get run over if you just sit there."

-Will Rogers

CHAPTER 8

The Greatest Gift

Life so often gives you the most incredible gift, brilliantly disguised as your worst nightmare.

In April 2014, I woke up, and my face felt strange. My lip felt tingly. When I put my hand upon my face, my lip was abnormally fat. Horrified, I looked in the mirror, and my face was hideous.

How did I get a fat lip, and only on one side of my mouth? Who in the world can say that? I racked my brain – *Did I hit my face in the middle of the night?* I couldn't figure out why in the world I had a half-fat lip.

I went into work feeling self-conscious about my lip – hiding my face with my hair. I went to my family doctor – he said I had a cold sore. Well, I knew it wasn't a cold sore. If it was – it was the mother of all cold sores.

I went to the dermatologist. He said that I should just get BOTOX to even out my lips. Feeling defeated, I went back to work and chatted with one of my co-workers. At this time, I worked for a place that manufactures dental equipment. My co-worker told me that he thought it was something dental-related. I couldn't figure out for the life of me how my fat lip could be dental-related. Finally, I agreed to see an endodontist, thinking I would need to have a root canal.

Have you ever had one of those moments in life when you wish someone were with you? I was reclining in the endodontist's chair, waiting for the doctor to come back and start the torturous root canal. Instead, he flips on the X-RAY screen, pulls up my charts, grabs the adjustable arm, and places the monitor right in front of my face. He proceeds to show me that I have a black mass the size of a golf ball on the left side of my mouth. I am grief-stricken. Breathe deep, Kathy, you've got this.

Well, that was three months of agony. I looked like a swollen mummy the day I had surgery to remove the tumor. To this day, I still have nerve pain on the left side of my face. Luckily the tumor was not cancerous.

As I was healing from my jaw tumor, I received the call and was told I had breast cancer. Being diagnosed with cancer can negatively affect your mental health and your mental health always affects your physical health. I never anticipated hearing those words from the other end of the phone. It had only been two weeks since I had had the tumor removed from my jaw. That jaw tumor was benign, so there was no way, in my mind, that I had breast cancer.

Have you ever had those events in life when you remember where you were when the event took place? That was me when I received the news that I had cancer. I recall the time of the day and what I was doing vividly. It was around 1:30 in the afternoon. I had been talking to an employee about one of her projects. Then, mid-conversation, my cell phone rang. I wasn't dreading the call as I expected that they were going to tell me the biopsy had come back normal. I answered the phone and the nurse ensured it was me by asking security questions and then says she needs to give the phone to the doctor. That made me curious. He proceeded to tell me that I had high-grade DCIS stage 0, which is cancer in the ducts. High-grade meaning if I didn't do something about it, then it would spread. I wrote the information on a tablet at work, trying to keep my composure as I was in the middle of my meeting. It didn't happen. I felt like a freight truck had just hit me. After a complicated and emotional three months of trying to figure out what was wrong with my jaw, now I have to deal with breast cancer? Uncontrollable tears were streaming down my face. I couldn't breathe and needed some fresh air. I went for a walk.

I had to watch a video that the nurse sent to me. The video is about breast cancer, the options for removal and what decisions needed to be made over the next few months as I learned more about my diagnosis. The video went into great detail about getting a mastectomy (removing the entire breast) or lumpectomy (removing the tumor), the surgery, and recovery. It also discussed the emotional pain of having surgery on the one thing that defines womanhood, your breast. Unless you have gone through cancer, I know many women and men reading this won't understand the true emotional impact of losing part of a breast. I know I didn't until I went through it.

It's an emotional roller coaster when you get told you have cancer. Questions were racing through my mind. What did I do wrong to get cancer? How did I get cancer? Are they sure? I was in the best health since I was a teenager and then got told I had cancer. How can that be? How can life be so unfair at times? When you have cancer, you don't have time to process your emotions, as the doctors want to initiate treatment as quickly as possible.

In August 2014, I had a lumpectomy. Following the surgery, I had six weeks of radiation. I started in September, and my celebration date was October 8th, 2014. Every day I would get my kids from school, head to the cancer center, and have my radiation done. The radiation made me incredibly tired. Two days a week, I would bring my son to basketball practice right after radiation. On those days, I would take a nap in the car while he was in the gym. The other days I just took a quick nap at home so I could function for the evening. The further along in the radiation I was, the more exhausted I became. I was fortunate as they caught mine so early that I didn't have to do chemo. Besides being tired, the radiation wasn't too unbearable until it ended. My body was burning from the inside out, my skin hurt to touch, my body ached when I moved, and I couldn't sleep. The left side of my face throbbed in pain because of jaw surgery. My right side hurt because of the lumpectomy and radiation.

My kids and I went on a celebration trip to Disneyland. I felt weird getting a disability pass and not standing in the horrendous lines. But, as my kids put it – "You shouldn't feel weird about it. You beat cancer." I still don't know how they truly felt during this whole year and me having cancer. They didn't talk much about it. I think they were trying to be strong for me.

My mentor, Les Brown, said, "Remember, life happens to all of us whether good or bad. We just need to find a way to grow through it."

Through your pain, you will find growth. I discovered that I had grown more spiritually during 2014 than any prior year. I was introduced to yoga and meditation that year, and my life hasn't been the same since. I learned how to calm my nerves, control my emotions, and live in the present. There is something sacred about the practice of yoga and meditation.

If you find yourself edgy and irritable, I urge you to attend a local yoga class or find one online. There are many free classes on YouTube. I would recommend being part of a class because there you will find community. There are many health benefits to yoga & meditation. John Hopkins medicine gives these non-spiritual benefits of yoga:

1. Yoga improves strength, balance, and flexibility.
2. Yoga helps with back pain relief.
3. Yoga can ease arthritis symptoms.
4. Yoga benefits heart health.
5. Yoga relaxes you to help you sleep better.

6. Yoga can mean more energy and brighter moods.

7. Yoga helps you manage stress.

8. Yoga connects you with a supportive community.

9. Yoga promotes better self-care.

Find a meditation practice that suits you. For some, it will be sitting quietly for a certain amount of time. For others, it will be a guided meditation. Some may prefer a walk in nature. Any of these practices are perfect. Whatever you choose will be perfect for you.

"Tears are words that need to be written."

-Paulo Coelho

CHAPTER 9

Chasing Happiness

As stated before, I didn't understand that happiness was an inside job. I thought someone, or something, else held the happiness for me. I have had to go through much heartache, hurt and healing to realize that HAPPY is me. It's that little girl that wants to be set free to run as fast as she can down a dirt road—this little girl who wants and needs to be loved unconditionally.

I had to figure out how to have fun again. I used to laugh all the time, and then life happened; degree after degree, climbing the corporate ladder, and being a mom. Now don't get me wrong; I love being a mom, working, and bettering myself. But, in those years, I was trying to be perfect, which meant I lost my joy in life.

I was faking my happiness so that others couldn't see the hurt that my soul was experiencing. It was easy for me to "fake" this happiness as I learned how to do it when I was a young child to protect myself from my unloving environment. I kept going to counselors, to motivational seminars, and reading books. I would be happy for a few weeks or possibly even a couple of months, but the emotions would always subside.

I took on more and more, whether at work, as a dance mom, or a basketball mom – the more I filled my life, the less I could feel my life. I was on the roller coaster of this healing journey, not realizing how to truly, and permanently, heal my heart.

I decided after my health issues in 2014 that I needed to quit taking life for granted. John Assaraf states, "Belief is the lens in which you see the world." I choose to look at the world through the lens of love, joy, and fun. Life is truly a gift. I realized that life is short; I needed to be happy now, as another day is not promised.

Life doesn't have to be perfect to be excellent. How low you've gone is how high you will rise. Life is a winding staircase with twists and turns and ups and downs. I thought I had to be in perfect health, have the ideal family, have the ultimate job and have the model house to be happy. For me, happiness was a destination, not a way of life. In my mind, I thought to myself, *When I get that next promotion, I will be happy. When I get the new car, I will be satisfied.* I didn't understand that happiness comes from within and not from the material things we accumulate or the people surrounding us.

Do you find yourself chasing your happiness or adding more into your life so you can escape? We are human beings who have become human doings. Quit being so busy as an excuse not to enjoy life and the beauty it has for us. If you could do anything today, what would it be? What is preventing you from doing it? Maybe it's calling a friend; perhaps it's planning a trip; maybe it's going for a walk, or perhaps it's as simple as taking a bath.

Do you feel happy? If not, why? Is your life out of balance? I find when I am out of balance; my soul needs to be in nature. Luckily, I live in Utah, so it's relatively easy for me to head up into the mountains. If you are in the city, do you go to the park? Do you watch the birds fly? Listen to them sing? Do you enjoy the different species of trees and all the other leaf formations? Do you put your feet in the grass like you did when you were a child? Do you play in the rain? That is one of my favorite things to do when it rains in the hot Utah summers. If it's raining, you will find me dancing in rain puddles in the middle of the street. Find one thing in nature that you find beautiful; breathe deeply and meditate on its beauty.

"Happiness is not something you postpone for the future; it is something you design for the present."

– Jim Rohn

CHAPTER 10

When we Heal,
those around us Heal

Talking about anxiety or depression used to be very difficult for me. Yet, people have asked me numerous times how, and why, I changed. I felt that it was appropriate to write this book for that person out there who needs to know they aren't alone, and maybe this book will help catapult them into a self-healing journey.

I changed because I was tired of living in depression, tired of blaming others, and tired of believing this was all that life had in store for me.

I changed by doing the work. I did each of the things that I have listed at the end of each chapter.

- I forgive.
- I apologize.
- I volunteer.
- I journal.
- I write gratitude lists.
- I write acknowledgment lists.

- I practice yoga.

- I meditate.

- I spend time in nature.

- I practice self-love.

- I have boundaries and abide by them.

If negative words are heard, these words make others feel small. Positive words encourage others to stand a little taller. Words have power. Our children will live with the results of what we said or didn't say. I am on a healing journey because I know if I heal myself, others around me heal.

Shelley Hitz wrote a book called" Broken crayons still color," a saying which I love. Think about a brand-new box of crayons and how each crayon is perfect. Each one has its special place in the box. The smell of a fresh new box of crayons relaxes you like you were a child ready to color that brand new page in a coloring book.

The box of crayons represents life and the possibilities that life can bring. But, unfortunately, life sometimes doesn't go as planned, and we feel broken. Sometimes we can be walking through life, and someone does something to us and brings brokenness into our lives. Sometimes, that brokenness comes from our own choices and our own decisions.

We all have those moments where we choose to do something, and we know what we are doing. We know the consequences and end up making mistakes and doing things we regret, and we wish we could go back and put those pieces back together.

And then sometimes life brings brokenness.

2007 brought my former father-in-law's death

2011 brought my mom's death

2011 brought divorce

2014 brought a jaw tumor

2014 brought breast cancer

2017 brought a torn ACL

2017 brought a house fire

I don't know where you are today. You may have had things done to you, you may have done something that you regret, or life may have just happened to you. No matter what has been done to you, no matter what you have done, no matter what life has brought you, broken crayons still color. Shattered mirrors still reflect light. Being broken does not mean that we are useless. Being shattered does not mean that we must be thrown out.

We have all had dreams in our lives, and then life got in our way and beat us up. So, rekindle your passion for life. Les Brown says, "If life knocks you down, if you can look up – you can get up." Don't define yourself where you are. Whatever you are going through is temporary. Stuff will happen in life. Focus on how you respond and focus each day on getting better, not bitter.

When we meet people, we create an impression. When we use our words, we create a difference. When we use our actions, we leave an imprint. So let's make sure we do things for the betterment of one another. My goal is to live a life that outlives me; spark a fire so deep and so bright that people will see it from far away.

To me, the definition of a warrior is the person who still fights inside to become the best version of themselves, no matter what life has given them in the past. So use these tools and unleash your inner warrior. The world needs you and is waiting.

You have time to be happy.

You have time to do whatever you want to do.

You are enough and always have been.

You have time to change your stars.

Bonus Section

30 Days of Self-Love

Day 1: Unplug for 10-15 minutes. Turn off your phone, computer, Kindle, gaming device, or television.

Day 2: Use Guided Meditation for 30 minutes prior to bed or first thing in the morning.

Day 3: Journal for 5 minutes.

Day 4: Clean one room in your house.

Day 5: Write 10 things that you are Grateful for.

Day 6: Drink 8 glasses of water.

Day 7: Don't spend any money today.

Day 8: Go for a walk outside.

Day 9: Soak in a Bubble Bath.

Day 10: Stretch for 10 minutes.

Day 11: Make a feel-good playlist.

Day 12: Dance for 10 minutes.

Day 13: Write down your To-Do's before going to bed.

Day 14: Make a List of 30 things that make you smile.

Day 15: Do an act of kindness for a stranger.

Day 16: What is on your bucket list? If you don't have one, make one.

Day 17: Write a letter to your future self. What would you want to know?

Day 18: Buy yourself flowers.

Day 19: Take a Nap.

Day 20: Call a friend and tell them how much they mean to you.

Day 21: Buy yourself one new piece of clothing.

Day 22: Take a relaxing hot shower.

Day 23: Write down a list of 10 things you love to do, such as going to the movies, traveling, etc. Plan and schedule your fun activities.

Day 24: Give out 5 complements today.

Day 25: Write a letter to your past self...what would you want to say?

Day 26: Write down your favorite quote (check bonus section for some amazing quotes).

Day 27: Read a chapter in a book.

Day 28: Try something new.

Day 29: Wake up 15 minutes earlier to give yourself extra "me-time."

Day 30: De-clutter your closet and donate the clothes you don't wear.

Self-Love Reflection
& Exercises

What does forgiveness mean to you?

_____

_____

_____

_____

_____

What are the benefits of forgiving?

_____

_____

_____

_____

_____

Are there situations where you need to forgive others or yourself? If yes, what are those situations? Let go and forgive something you or someone else has done in the past.

_____

_____

_____

_____

_____

How can you be more compassionate towards yourself?

_____

_____

_____

_____

_____

Think about an experience where you gave your power away to someone else.

_____

_____

_____

_____

_____

- *How did you feel during that time?*

_____

_____

_____

_____

- *What practices can you put in place to protect yourself from a similar situation in the future?*

_____

_____

_____

_____

_____

Hug yourself and tell yourself how amazing you are.

> *Write down how that made you feel. For a lot of us, it will feel fake and that we are unworthy. If that's your first thought, try some other types of affirmations such as "I am worthy to love myself."*

_____

_____

_____

_____

_____

Write down 10 things that you love about yourself. Read these 10 things aloud in front of the mirror and try to feel the love within.

1._____

2._____

3._____

4._____

5._____

6._____

7._____

8._____

9._____

10._____

A limiting belief is a belief that you have about yourself that is not necessarily true. On the left side, write down your limiting beliefs about yourself. On the right side of the page, write down where these beliefs came from. More than likely, they have come from some experience you had as a child.

My Limiting Beliefs   *Where did these beliefs come from?*

_____

_____

_____

_____

_____

_____

_____

_____

_____

_____

_____

_____

Write a love letter to yourself. Include all the things that you appreciate about yourself. Write by hand so it can be as personal and loving as possible. Show love and compassion towards yourself. Apologize and accept your flaws. We all have them so let's accept them. Be positive and thank yourself.

_____

_____

_____

_____

_____

_____

_____

_____

_____

_____

_____

_____

_____

What is fear to you?

_____

_____

_____

_____

_____

What am I afraid of?

_____

_____

_____

_____

- *What will happen if this doesn't go the way I anticipated?*

_____

_____

_____

_____

What three things are you most proud of in your life to date?

1._____

2._____

3._____

What do you hope to achieve in life?

_____

_____

_____

_____

_____

If you could accomplish only one thing before you died, what would it be?

_____

_____

_____

_____

_____

For the next thirty days, write out ten items you are grateful for daily and ten items you want to acknowledge yourself for daily. Gratitude usually is for something outside of yourself, while acknowledgments are things that occur through you. For example, I am grateful for my house, food, and electricity. I acknowledge myself for writing this book.

_____

_____

_____

_____

_____

_____

_____

_____

_____

_____

_____

_____

_____

Write about one person who inspires you and why.

_____

_____

_____

_____

_____

Walk for at least 10 minutes daily. Exercise distracts you from negative thoughts and helps overcome anxiety and depression. Write about how you felt before, during, and after.

_____

_____

_____

_____

_____

_____

_____

_____

_____

Get clear with something you desire. Imagine for 10 minutes living this desired life.

Make a list of everything you do in a day and write down why you do it. This will help you identify what's most important and whether you are spending your time with it.

_____

_____

_____

_____

_____

_____

_____

_____

_____

_____

_____

_____

_____

_____

Make a list of your daily emotions. On the left side write down your emotions, listed by the hour, the right side should detail the context that surrounded that emotion. Once you've listed all emotions, start to compare, and analyze them. What's the ratio of positive vs. negative emotions? Which emotions dominate and what causes them? What are their triggers?

_____

_____

_____

_____

_____

_____

_____

_____

_____

_____

_____

_____

_____

_____

Notice how you are breathing. Are you taking enough breaths? When we get stressed; we tend to hold our breath. It's a coping mechanism we learned as children. Are you holding your breath? Are you breathing in the chest? Are you breathing fully through your stomach? If you take a big breath and push out your tummy, this will relax you. Do this 10 times when you feel stress coming on.

_____

_____

_____

_____

_____

When in a stressful situation; before you react, think! Take 10 deep breaths or even better, take a sip of water, then respond. This will help you avoid snapping by calming yourself down.

_____

_____

_____

_____

_____

Be Present with your family, your co-workers, and friends. Because life is so busy for all of us, we try to multi-task every moment we can. How many times have you been in a meeting, and someone is typing away at their keyboard instead of paying attention to the speaker? First, it's rude and second, it's not productive. Whatever situation it is, just be present, don't think about the past or the future, fully experience what is happening now.

We tend to get so stuck in our own worlds that we fail to notice what is happening around us. When you are at the office or even at home, observe the behavior around you. When do people walk around and go to speak to others. Who do they talk to? What are their moods? How are their desks arranged? What are individuals feeling? What is the group mood overall? What do you see and hear? (Don't stalk them but be observant).

Make sure to say, "thank you," "please," and "I'm Sorry" to those people closest to you.

_____

_____

_____

_____

Remember other people's names as this means the world to them. It shows you are paying attention and that you care.

_____

_____

_____

_____

Quotes To Live By

- *The ones who notice the storms in your eyes, the silence in your voice and the heaviness in your heart are the ones you need to let in.*

  - Unknown

- *"It is never too late to be what you might have been."*
  -George Elliott

- *"Excuse me, Your Life Is Waiting."*
  -Lynn Grabhorn

- *"We don't learn from experiences, we learn from reflecting on the experience."*
  -John Dewey

- *"A happy life is one which is in accordance with its own nature."*
  – Seneca

- *"There is no path to happiness: happiness is the path."*
  -Buddha

- *"Do not learn to react. Learn how to respond."*
  -Buddha

- *"There is a calmness to a life lived in gratitude, a quiet joy."*
  -Ralph H. Blum

- *"Create the life you can't wait to wake up to."*
  — Josie Spinardi

- *"Sometimes you have to get off track to discover a better track."*
  -Robin Sharma

- *"Fear is the path to the Dark Side. Fear leads to anger, anger leads to hate, hate leads to suffering."*
  – Yoda

- *"A Life Lived In Fear Is Half Lived"*
  Baz Luhrmann

- *"When you don't have the strength to take another step, ask those you love to pull you."*
  — Unknown

- *"The epic story of tomorrow can't be written if it ends today."*
  — Unknown

- *"To fall in love with yourself is the first secret to happiness."*
  -Robert Morley

- *"The best preparation for tomorrow is doing your best today."*
  H. Jackson Brown, Jr.

- *"Change your thoughts and you change your world."*
  Norman Vincent Peale

- *"The only limits you have are the limits you believe."*
  Wayne Dyer

Affirmations

I love myself.

I am kind.

I am confident in all that I do.

I am doing the best that I can.

I believe in myself.

I accept myself.

I am smart.

I am capable.

I am beautiful.

I am present in this moment.

I am a good and kind person.

I take care of myself.

I am a unique and interesting person.

I am empathic to those around me.

I deserve the best.

I am focused on my own well-being.

I am in touch with my inner being.

I am grateful.

I have beautiful qualities to offer this world.

I deserve to be appreciated.

I am strong.

I am proud of who I am.

I am stronger because of my struggles.

I am enough.

I am attracting positive experiences in my life.

I achieve my goals.

I follow my heart.

I am confident.

I am blessed.

I deserve peace.

Resources

https://www.iliyanastareva.com/blog/emotional-intelligence-exercises

https://cindypowersprosor.com/wp-content/uploads/2017/02/30-self-love-challenge.jpg

CPSIA information can be obtained
at www.ICGtesting.com
Printed in the USA
LVHW030524130522
718142LV00004B/9